How to Pick a Fort

Contents

Written by Rob Alcraft

Collins

How to pick a fort

A good fort is hard to attack.
It is hard to get near.

Attackers need a boat to get to this fort!

Towers

Look for high towers.
Then you can see
attackers far off!

tower

A good fort is solid. It is hard to bash apart.

Go zig-zag!

Zig-zag forts are fantastic.
Attackers will not get in.

Dig deep

Look for pits and moats to put attackers off.

moat

ramparts of rock and soil

Keep food

Attacks might go on for weeks.
Keep loads of food – and gunpowder.

hidden room

gunpowder

food

Boom and bang!

You will need to load cannons to fight off raiders.

13

Be a winner

Pick the right fort and you can keep it!

solid

hard to get near

cannons

15

A fort

keep

tower

moat

ramparts

Pick a fort!

Pick posh or solid?

Posh

Cool and high up ☆☆☆

Solid

Wet! ⭐⭐⭐

Dark! ⭐⭐⭐

Did you get it right?

Fail

This posh tower fell down!

Winner

This fort is solid!

How to pick a fort

🐾 Review: After reading 🐾

Use your assessment from hearing the children read to choose any GPCs, words or tricky words that need additional practice.

Read 1: Decoding

- Point to **loads** on page 10. Discuss its meaning in context. (*lots of food*) Point to **load** on page 12. Ask: Does this have a similar meaning? Discuss it in context and explain how **load** here means "fill" (*fill the cannons*).

- Ask the children to read pages 8 and 9. How many digraphs can they find, which each make one sound? (*d<u>ee</u>p, **L<u>oo</u>k**, m<u>oa</u>ts, a<u>tt</u>ackers, ramp<u>ar</u>ts*)

- Point to labels and encourage the children to read the words fluently. Say: Can you blend in your head when you read these words?

Read 2: Prosody

- Turn to the contents page and challenge the children to each read a heading. Say: Read like a salesperson. Make your heading sound like the most important or exciting page in the book!

- Discuss which words to emphasise in order to draw the listener in, for example, **deep**, **winner** and **keeps**.

- Encourage them to try out a different pace or tone too, in order to sound more persuasive.

Read 3: Comprehension

- Encourage the children to describe forts they have visited or seen on TV programmes or in films. Would they like to live in one? Why or why not?

- Hold a discussion on what makes the best fort, using information from the text. Ask:

  o What are the most important features it should have? (e.g. *hard to get near, solid, walls, towers, cannons, etc*)

- Turn to pages 22–23 and talk about all the different features of good forts. Ask the children to pick a fort to talk about. Ask: Which fort would you choose and why?

- Bonus content: Turn to pages 18 and 19 and discuss the words **Posh** and **Solid**.

  o Ask: What do they mean in this context? (e.g. *Posh: elegant, with lots of towers*; *Solid: well-built, thick-walled*)